THE QUEST FOR A
"NATIONAL" NATIONALISM

THE QUEST

FOR A

"NATIONAL"
NATIONALISM

E. J. PRATT'S EPIC AMBITION,
"RACE" CONSCIOUSNESS,
AND THE CONTRADICTIONS
OF CANADIAN IDENTITY

GEORGE ELLIOTT CLARKE

BREAKWATER
P.O. Box 2188, St. John's, NL, Canada, A1C 6E6
www.breakwaterbooks.com

COPYRIGHT © 2021 George Elliott Clarke
ISBN 978-1-55081-875-8
A CIP catalogue record for this book is available from
Library and Archives Canada

The main typeface used throughout this book is Adobe
Jenson Pro. Adobe Jenson Pro captures the essence of
Nicolas Jenson's roman and Ludovico degli Arrighi's italic
typeface designs. The combined strength and beauty of these
two icons of Renaissance type result in an elegant typeface
suited to a broad spectrum of applications. Designed by
Robert Slimbach, Adobe Jenson Pro provides a power and
flexibility for text composition rarely found in digital type.

We acknowledge the support of the Canada Council
for the Arts. We acknowledge the financial support of the
Government of Canada through the Department of Heritage
and the Government of Newfoundland and Labrador
through the Department of Tourism, Culture, Arts and
Recreation for our publishing activities.

PRINTED AND BOUND IN CANADA.

Breakwater Books is committed to choosing papers and
materials for our books that help to protect our environment.
To this end, this book is printed on recycled paper that is
certified by the Forest Stewardship Council®.

For Boyd Warren Chubbs,
Lyric Bard of Labrador

POUND AND FRYE

IN 1909, responding to maternal musing on the idea of an "Epic of the West" (Moody 121), the European-American poet Ezra Pound propounds four determinants for an American epic:

1. a beautiful tradition.
2. a unity in the outline of that tradition vid. The Odyssey.
3. a Hero—mythical or historical.
4. a dam [sic] long time for the story to loose [sic] its gharish [sic] detail & get encrusted with a bunch of beautiful lies. (qtd in Moody 121)

Pound declares that Henry Wadsworth Longfellow "tried to hist [sic] up an amerikan [sic] epik [sic]" (qtd in Moody 121), referring, presumably, to his *Evangeline: A Tale of Acadie* (1847), which tells the story of two lovers separated nearly unto death due to the British Expulsion of the Acadians from Nova Scotia in 1755, or to his *The Song of Hiawatha* (1855), retelling Ojibway legends. But, for Pound, Longfellow could not be a pre-eminent precursor because America itself "has no mysterious & shadowy past to make her interesting" (qtd in Moody 122), while the present is all money-grubbing. Pound theorizes that the would-be epic poet "needs figures to move on the epic stage & they have to be men who are more than men, with sight more than mansight" (the latter neologism suggests they should possess supernatural or divine insight), and "They have to be picturesque" (qtd in Moody 122). For those who might nominate Walt Whitman and his *Leaves of Grass* (1855) as an American epic, Pound retorts that that poetry collection is merely "interesting as ethnology" (qtd in Moody 122). Clearly, for him, the effective epic poem cannot focus on minorities—Acadian or Ojibway—or even utilize the miscellaneous speech of the variegated citizens of the United States of America. Heteroglossia, he sniffs, cannot provide the model for the epic.[1] To repulse his mother's notion of the American epic, Pound moves, impishly, that only "a religion of 'Chivalry in affairs of money,'" with

---

[1] Of course, Pound's own epic, *The Cantos*, is festively heteroglossic.

a lingo, presumably, of stocks and mortgages, could inform an American poem of high purpose (qtd in Moody 122). Ideally, Pound elaborates, the American epic poet must be one who "will walk very much alone, with his eyes on the beauty of the past of the old world, or on the glory of a spiritual kingdom, or on some earthly new Jerusalem—which might as well be upon Mr Shackletons antarctic [sic] ice fields as in Omaha.... Canada, Australia, New Zeland [sic], South Africa, set your hypothetical [epic] where you like" (qtd in Moody 122). The trouble is, Yanks lack the ethnic and national unity of the Portuguese poet Luís Vaz de Camões,[2] who Pound feels "is the only man who ever did a nearly contemporary subject with any degree of success & [who] had the line of [explorer] Vasco de Gamas voyage for unity... & the mythical history of Portugal for back ground [sic]" (qtd in Moody 122). Bereft of such homogeneity, the American poet must either babble polyphonously, Pound suspects, or "parley Euphues"—that is to say, slither out

---

[2] His *The Lusiads* (1572) relates Portuguese history to both biblical and Greek heroic poetry. Yet, Camões's text is stridently racist so as to justify Portuguese imperialism versus non-whites and non-Christians. In a typical confrontation, the Portuguese—"not men to suffer [Moslem] dogs to show their teeth"—cannonade the foe, and follow up "the victory with more killing and destruction..." (52-53).

the silver-tongue of commerce (qtd in Moody 123). Ultimately, Pound resolves, "An epic in the real sense is the speech of a nation thru the mouth of one man" (qtd in Moody 122). He stresses unities—of 'race' ("nation"), rhetoric ("the speech of a nation"), and the 'individual talent' ("one man"). Almost a decade on, in 1917-1918, Pound holds that heteroglossia, or many-mouthed hubbub, cannot produce the epic voice, which must be national and haughty, imperial: In a letter to his father, Homer, Pound alleges that the merely local, or, in his terms, American, is a backwater of the British canon (Moody 330). What Pound designates as provincial is almost always the ethnic, the minority, the ex-central (eccentric), and the marginal....

Is Pound wrong? Generally, the epic answers the question "Who are we?" Surely, that answer's found most readily if the poet is treating a singular, cultural entity, and one exuding mythic or imaginative force. Canadian critic Northrop Frye says as much when he asserts that the epic poet may attempt "a single encyclopaedic form," descended from "a total body of vision," if he is "sufficiently learned or inspired" (55). The epic may also originate— as a set of communal, oracular verses— "by a poetic school or tradition if the culture is sufficiently homogeneous" (55). Yet, the epic poet, being "a spokesman of his society," and explicitly *not* of "a second society" (54)—that is, a minority group or a colonial people, finds articulated in himself "a poetic knowledge and expressive power which is latent or needed in his society..." (54). Even so, civilizations themselves may birth "traditional tales and myths and histories [that] have a strong tendency to stick together and form encyclopaedic aggregates" (55-56), such as, Frye credits, is true for the Homeric epics and the Finnish *Kalevala*, too, even though "everything that is unified or continuous about the poem is a nineteenth-century reconstruction" (56). Frye seconds Pound, then, in finding that epic is the voice of a civilization (or a culture), the vocalization of a unity of cultural experience, and he also senses that the form itself "makes some attempt to preserve the convention of recitation and a listening audience" (248). Frye also echoes Pound in disparaging the 'provincial': "The province or region ... is usually a vestigial curiosity to be written up by some nostalgic tourist" ("Canada" 89). One should not conceive such a limited or narrow space capable of supporting the epic imagination: Frye insists, then, that "culture seems to flourish best in national units ... the empire is too big and the province too small for major literature" ("Canada" 89).

Given these existential limitations for Canadian poetry, its provincial and colonial inheritance, and its bifurcated national voice (French and English), it should be difficult for Canada to produce epic poets. But Frye elects one: E. J. Pratt; and one Pratt poem, namely, *Brébeuf and His Brethren* (1940). For Frye, "Canadian poetry is at its best a poetry of incubus and *cauchemar*," featuring "Nature … consistently sinister and menacing," and so the martyrdom of the French Jesuit priest Brébeuf yields "the greatest single Canadian poem" ("Canada" 96-97). Herein, "the man with the vision beyond nature is tied to the stake and destroyed by savages who are in the state of nature, and who represent its mindless barbarity" ("Canada" 97). While Frye's account of the poem posits a classic racialism, where European Christian civilization is crucified by North American heathens, unenlightened and irrational, Frye also notes shrewdly, "the black-coated figure at the stake is also a terrifying devil to the savages, *Echon*, the evil one" ("Canada" 97). Despite this arguably noble moral relativism, Frye imposes the standard reading of Canadian colonial history: Indigenous Canadians are doomed savages, fated to endure as much justified annihilation as will—a few centuries on—the progenitors of Nazism ("Canada" 97).

Clearly, both Pound and Frye assess twentieth-century epic as requiring an ethnocentric and/or nationalist poetic through which the epic poet appears as the vatic articulator of the dominant—or administrating—ethnicity of a nation or imperial homeland. Playfully, Pound pretends that the true, unifying language of the United States is that of Wall Street and Madison Avenue, commerce and slogans. Yet, his own epic, *The Cantos* (1917-1987),[3] executes just such bombastic crud, while also exploiting a miscellany of ugly, ethnic caricatures (particularly of Jews). For his part, Frye elects Pratt English Canada's great epic poet, thanks to a poem that represents the implantation of European Christianity upon Canadian soil and its displacement of Indigenous civilization, cast as regressive barbarism.[4]

---

[3] *The Cantos* is a challenge to date. Even so, the Faber & Faber Fourth Collection Edition (1987) is a legitimate, belated tombstone for Pound's epic, which ended, definitively, with the author's death in 1972. Pound's first "Three Cantos" appeared in *Poetry* in 1917.

[4] In his study of *The Cantos*, Peter Stoicheff remarks that Pound allows a "backward glance"—or pseudo-revisionist statement—at the conclusion of his epic because he seeks to return "to a point in the poem and his career free of ... particular overt, and covert, political and racist voices" (8). Stoicheff argues that like questioning afflicts "other long poems of the twentieth century" (8). However, Pratt does not indulge such introspection in *Brébeuf*.

PRATT'S *BRÉBEUF*

THESE provisos of Pound and Frye tutor E. J. Pratt's tyro attempt at an epic—or, simply, long—poem, *Brébeuf and His Brethren* (1940), which Sandra Djwa sees as having been "a parable for a nation then at war" (xvii), providing, she attests, "a moral for the wartime present and [bringing] together Canada's national past of French and English, Catholic and Protestant, priests and natives" (xvii). Djwa understands that the poem "hints obliquely at the Second World War in [its] account of the wars of the Huron and Iroquois in seventeenth-century New France" (xvi), while also drawing ironic juxtapositions, here and there, between "priest and native," given that both the supposedly civilized French and the supposedly savage Indigenous peoples are capable of applying torture (xvii). Djwa establishes, nevertheless, that "the poem's controlling antithesis becomes that of 'savage' (heathen) versus 'civilized' Christian" (xvii). One may tease out an implicit allegory positioning the barbarians as prototype Nazis and the French martyrs as prototype Allies (who, in 1940, were all but routed on continental Europe, with the Soviet Union still a German ally and Britain undergoing aerial bombardment). To any impartial analyst, in 1939-40, the Allies—who were, principally, France, Britain (plus their colonies), and the Dominions (including Canada)— must have appeared probable martyrs themselves, given the impossible campaign of British forces—with Canadian troops alongside—to help France fight off Germany in May 1940. Djwa is correct to read Pratt's epyllion or mini-epic as subtle propaganda intended to nudge Canadian readers to stay the course, whatever the cost, in the Anti-Fascist War.

However, *Brébeuf* is no serious attempt at "national" epic, despite Djwa's assertion that Pratt believed that "Canadian poets had not yet provided a sense of national myth" (xvi), even if such mythopoesis (to use a Frygian term) is the special *raison d'être* of the epic poet. For one thing, the poem ignores English Canada, I mean, all the British (North) American colonies and colonists. Though it is writ, obviously, in English, its heroes are

French Catholic priests, nobly striving to spread Christianity and "Enlightenment" to unreasoning and unreasonable heathen. Yes, the immediate audience for *Brébeuf* was English. Clearly, the poem means to urge liberal-democratic Christians to confront Fascism in its German—and let's add Italian and Japanese—formations. But English-Canadians, who backed the war effort—and manned it—did not require the coded lecture. Nor is the poem a prayer for Catholic and Protestant unity. Protestants—and Protestantism—are utterly immaterial to *Brébeuf*. Pratt's—the poem's—focus is on Catholic intervention, French Catholic martyrdom—in Christianizing and civilizing the uncouth, *de facto* anti-Christians of the colonial wilderness. But why?

The most compelling context for the drafting of Pratt's wartime poem is, I wager, his memory of the quarrel over conscription—or the draft—that divided French and English Canadians bitterly in World War I and, in 1939-40, threatened to do so again during World War II. During the Great War, Pratt pondered the horrific obliteration of the Newfoundland Regiment at Beaumont-Hamel, France, on July 1, 1916 (Pitt 159). Indeed, the annihilation of these colonial

Newfoundlanders inspired Pratt to "commit his pen 'to the Cause'" (Pitt 160), thus falling "victim to the war fever," states biographer David G. Pitt, and writing "almost nothing but war verse for nearly the next two years," that is, 1916-18 (165). Because Pratt was a conscious witness to the trials, tribulations, and trauma of the Great War, and because he had become, by 1907, a student at Victoria College and, thus, a citizen of Toronto, he must needs have experienced the Conscription Crisis that beset the Dominion of Canada, 1917-18. (The Crisis was a result of the slaughter of Canadian volunteer servicemen in the Battle of the Somme [July 1-November 18, 1916], the same battle that had destroyed the Newfoundland Regiment.) Indeed, in "desperate need" for more troops, and faced with the failure of a recruitment drive in Quebec, the Government of Canada turned to conscription as the solution ("Conscription Crisis of 1917"). Thus, the Dominion was riven "between English-speaking imperialists who supported the overseas war effort and French-speaking nationalists who believed that conscription was a second attempt to impose the Conquest [of 1760], therefore it needed to be resisted at all costs" ("Conscription Crisis of 1917"). Francophone Québécois opposition to conscription was passionate enough that riots, allegedly involving thousands, erupted in Montreal between March 28 and April 1, 1918, where a conscription registration office was sacked, while two pro-conscription newspapers in Quebec City saw their offices vandalized ("Conscription Crisis of 1917"). Having witnessed the grievous sundering of French and English Canadians in the Great War, Pratt had reason to fear a repeat of ethnic tensions when the Second World War came to pass. Then again, not only had French-Canadian nationalism persisted, but, in the 1920s-30s, it had also absorbed a pro-Fascist, pro-Nazi, and anti-Semitic element. By the time the new global war broke out, states historian Jean-François Nadeau, *"Les fascistes canadiens s'opposent farouchement à la guerre qui s'annonce en Europe, ainsi qu'à la participation éventuelle du Canada"* (251). This opposition was not inconsequential. Maintains Nadeau, on January 6, 1939, English-born Toronto lawyer Joseph Sedgwick warned a Rotary Club audience that Canadian (Québécois) Fascist leader Adrien Arcand *"est aussi puissant au Canada que Mussolini l'était en Italie en 1920 ou qu'Hitler le devenait à compter de 1929"* (249).

Perhaps most intriguingly for Pratt, French-Canadian Fascism found it sporting to utilize

Indigenous symbols. For instance, the Franco-phone Fascist organ, *Le Goglu*, in its edition of January 6, 1933, published a cartoon illustrating an uprising by Iroquois at Kahnawake/Caughnawaga, protesting the hiring of immigrant workers to construct the Mercier Bridge (Nadeau 74-76). Despite the contemporary, industrial setting of bridge construction, the cartoonist illustrates the violent Iroquois anachronistically as bare-chested stick-brandishers and tomahawk-wielders, their abs and/or biceps emblazoned with swastika tattoos (Nadeau 75). The cartoon salutes the Iroquois for resorting to Aryan-style force to assert their natural rights. Historian Nadeau observes that German Nazism admired the Sioux Nation for its supposed subscription to a militant assertion of their noble purity, and so enrolled the Sioux as *"membres honoraires de la grande famille aryenne"* (Nadeau 76). In addition, when the swashbuckling Italian Fascist, airman, and man-of-state Italo Balbo (1896-1940) led a squadron of Italian aviators on a trans-Atlantic, North American tour in 1933, 15,000 people came out to greet him in the Francophone-dominated Acadian town of Shediac, New Brunswick, while another large crowd celebrated him in suburban Montreal (145-152). Most vitally—upon arrival in Chicago, Balbo was made an honorary Sioux chief (Nadeau 152).

Given the provincial, 1930s, allegorical *ménage à trois* conjoining Fascism, French-Canadian nationalism, and Indigenous militancy, one understands why Pratt, in approaching the writing of *Brébeuf*, felt moved to muse on the correspondence between Indigenous "savagery" and Fascist oratory:

> [W]hat a dramatic study would be the face of a chief when he was whipping up his tribe to a war fever. As the language didn't have any labials the mouth would have to be kept wide open all the time of the harangue. What an illumination upon modern totalitarian oratory. Some reporter described Mussolini as unable to make a speech without showing all his back teeth. (Qtd in Gingell 125-126)

It is this ideological necessity to present Fascists in the guise of Natives that prods Pratt, I speculate, to animalize the heathen that the seventeenth-century French missionaries confront, and he does so zealously, or with apt gusto. Thus, the Catholic priests encounter "the swarm / of hostile Iroquois" (*Brébeuf* l.186-187), and the modifying noun aligns them with insects or a pack of predators.

Even pacific (or pacified) Natives—Hurons—who join the French in their missions are said to arrive "swarming" (l.1777). Later, we are asked to view the Indigenous people, the Iroquois, as, in reality, "Infesting" the Canadian wilderness, a verb that exiles them as outsiders and as disease, as cancers (l.1699). Elsewhere, we read that "the native mood / Was hostile" (*Brébeuf* l.422-423), which could be a nod to the persistent sabre-rattling, throughout the 1930s, of Hitler versus England and Mussolini versus Ethiopia. When Pratt casts "The noisy pack of Indians" (*Brébeuf* l.496) as "barbarians" who are a diabolical inverse of "Aristotle and Saint Thomas" (l.755-756), and "A race so unlike men" (l.802), one must expect "A brave" (l.1140) to express a cannibal creed: "'I have had enough,' he said, / 'Of the dark flesh of my enemies. I mean / To kill and eat the white flesh of the priests'" (l.1142-1144). Certainly, Pratt's Natives are nasty sadists, for whom "fears and prejudices / [Haunt] the shadows of their racial past" (l.889-890). "[B]arbarous / In birth and manners" (l.1206-1207), the enemy Indigenous anticipate the tactics of Nazi storm troopers, for they've "stormed" Huron villages (l.1777).

Yes, this racialization—and Nazification—of Indigenous peoples who reject Caucasian,

Christian civilization is, undoubtedly, intellectually shoddy—as much an act of propaganda, really, as any libel or slander published or broadcast by the Axis powers. Yet, Pratt decides that he must depict the historical Iroquois as akin to contemporary Fascists, for Caucasians do not need convincing that non-Caucasians are evil (or sinful);[5] nor do White Anglo-Saxon Protestants require reassurance about the virtues of facing off against "restless Natives" and/or ruthless Nazis. Rather, it is French-Canadian Catholics—lukewarm about the virtues of the Anti-Fascist War and an audience cool to boasts about Anglo-Saxon "greatness"—who need reminding that they, too, if they honour the martyrdom of their missionary forebears, need shoulder not a Kiplingesque "White Man's Burden" but that of Democracy versus Tyranny. Thus, the poem opens with the curious notice that "The winds of God were blowing over France" (*Brébeuf* l.1), a weather event, apparently, that prods French priests to exchange tolerable, European monasteries for mosquito-pestered, *Nouvelle-France* canoes.

---

[5] Witness Frantz Fanon's *bons mots*: "In the collective unconscious of the *homo occidentalis*, the Negro—or, if one prefers, the color black—symbolizes evil, sin, wretchedness, death, war, famine" (*Black* 190-191).

Writing about writing *Brébeuf*, Pratt observes, the historical priests had "chances … again and again" to "get out" and return to France, but he was, he says, "struck by the number of times the priests in the Huron country renewed their vows" (qtd in Gingell 123). To draw the parallel in bold ink, Pratt implies that the latest "Brethren" of the French Brébeuf, currently being summoned to be steadfast, endure, and offer themselves as martyrs, are, *oui*, French Canadians. However, now they are expected not to perish in testifying to pagan Natives, but to perhaps sacrifice themselves in the crusade against Fascism (and militarism), that is to say, in what Pratt's speaker labels "the cause of France" (*Brébeuf* l.1362). In 1940, when the poem got published, there was one overriding "cause"—at least for de Gaulle's Free French forces—namely, to see France liberated from German Nazi rule. This fight appealed to Anglophones, but not Francophone Canadians, who, as in 1917, "felt that they had no particular loyalty to either Britain or France" ("Conscription Crisis of 1917"). Given this reality, Pratt repeats the phrase the "winds of God" at *Brébeuf*'s conclusion (l.2115), in a coda that abandons the Miltonic blank verse of most of the previous 2020 lines to adopt a freer form. Significantly, the last 30 lines of the poem assume the present tense:

"Three hundred years have passed, and the winds of God / Which blew over France are blowing once more through the pines / That bulwark the shores of the great Fresh Water Sea" (l.2115-2117). Furthermore, this coda addresses a present-day "Martyrs' Shrine" (109), *circa* 1940, on the presumed site of the celebrated, European/Catholic hecatombs. Evidently, the original divine summons to missionary sacrifice, which brought the French to *Nouvelle-France* centuries ago, is now "blowing" through Canadian pines, presumably to spur present-day French-Canadians—the descendants of Brébeuf's brethren (if not of the chaste and celibate and, thus, sterile Brébeuf himself)—to take up the cross of Enlightened Humanitarianism and eliminate Nazi barbarism and, not coincidentally, liberate France—the homeland—from *les hitlériens*.

If *Brébeuf* is pro-war, pro-Francophone-enlistment propaganda, togged up as a paean to ye olde Christian missionary slaughter, another Pratt poem, one that appears in Ralph Gustafson's edited *Anthology of Canadian Poetry (English)* (1942), but also in *Complete Poems Part I* (1989), is pertinent here. I refer to Pratt's "From Stone to Steel," and in particular its lines, "The snarl Neanderthal is worn / Close to the smiling Aryan lips" (l.5-6).

Clearly, this couplet, apparently first published in 1936,[6] anticipates *Brébeuf*, with Indigenous warriors representing both the "Neanderthal" and the latter-day "Aryan." (One spies again Pratt's acknowledgment of the Fascist tendency to align putative Amerindian bloodthirstiness with Aryan machismo.)

Of course, "From Stone to Steel" concludes with a reference to Christ's accepting, at Gethsemane, the agony of martyrdom. Through His example, otherwise naturally diabolical human beings are inspired to acquire humanitarianism, liberal democracy, and charity:

> The road goes up, the road goes down—
> Let Java or Geneva be—
> But whether to the cross or crown,
> The path lies through Gethsemane.
> (l.17-20)

Note that *Brébeuf* ends similarly, aligning the courage of the French priests with that of Christ Himself, whose martyrdom involves "the sound of invisible trumpets blowing / Around two slabs of board, right-angled, hammered / By Roman nails and hung on a Jewish

---

[6]   Originally entitled "From Java to Geneva," the verses appear in *New Provinces: Poems of Several Authors*, by E. J. Pratt, et al., 1936, rpt. Toronto: University of Toronto Press, 1976, p. 44.

hill" (l.2068-2070). Again, Pratt's argument
is—I'll be colloquial— "Yo, Frenchies, Papists,
die like Christ, to rescue France—and, well,
the British Empire and a Protestant King."

"From Stone to Steel"—included in Gustafson's weaponization of Anglo-Canadian verse
(I refer to his production of an anthology
distributed to Canuck troops [*Anthology*
58-59])—pursues a generic project of anti-
Axis bellicosity, as opposed to the Francophone-oriented project of *Brébeuf*. (Note
that Gustafson laboured on behalf of British
Information Services, 1942-46, a New York
City–based sponsor of British propaganda.[7])
Printed in a Penguin / Pelican pocket-book,
suitable for a soldier's kit, the poem is access-
ible for any Maple-Leaf-branded soldiery.
However, if *Brébeuf* was intended for a wartime,
Francophone readership, ideally, it required
a French translation. Yet, no French-Canadian
translation was produced until 1988, by
Patricia Godbout, who explains, in the abstract
to her work, *Brébeuf et ses frères*:

> what drew my attention to that
> particular poem was the fact that
> Pratt, an English Protestant, had
> decided to devote his longest poem

---

[7]   See "Ralph Gustafson."

to a Catholic Frenchman, to whom only a few lines would normally be devoted in an English history textbook. As Henry Wells puts it, one singular aspect of *Brebeuf* [sic] *and his Brethren* is the fact that it is "the story of Roman Catholics told by a Protestant, the story of Frenchmen told by an English Canadian." (Abstract, *Brébeuf et ses frères*)

In other words, Godbout is drawn to the poem for precisely one of the reasons that Pratt chose to write it—that is, for its attempt to represent the "nation" of Canada, ideally, to project Canadian nationalism as the instance of the fraternal embrace of Francophone Catholics by an Anglophone Protestant. As such, Pratt must have hoped that his poem would see translation into French quite readily. Perhaps he prayed that his poem would be, if not translated, at least "overheard" in French Canada, to use a concept that Philip Brian Harper employs in his 1993 argument that white audiences "*overheard*" Black American protest poetry of the 1960s. Critically, given the absence of a translation, the Québécois-troop-recruitment inclinations of the poem could only be effective if they were "overheard" by Francophones.

Yet, given that Pratt was "the principal Canadian poet from 1923 to 1955," as Djwa attests (xii), and allowing that his "reputation as a poet stands higher than that of most other poets in English Canada," as Godbout opines (Abstract, *Brébeuf et ses frères*), Pratt would have had reason to expect that, like another English poet who appealed to Francophone Catholic Canadians, namely, Henry Wadsworth Longfellow, his Francophone-oriented poem would attain translation. Surely, Pratt would have recognized that Longfellow's *Evangeline* (1847) had been adopted by French-Canadians, especially *les Acadiens*, as a "national epic," even though it was imagined by an Anglophone and written by an American. The popularity of *Evangeline* in French Canada was due to a translation authored by Pamphile LeMay, in 1865, 18 years after the poem's issuance in English. Pratt was tempted, I wager, to prophesize a similar success.

So, Pratt follows Longfellow in appropriating a tale from *Nouvelle-France* and employing it to create 'national' myth. Here are Longfellow's opening lines:

> This is the forest primeval. The murmuring pines and the hemlocks,
> Bearded with moss, and in garments green, indistinct in the twilight,

> Stand like Druids of eld, with voices sad
> and prophetic,
> Stand like harpers hoar, with beards that
> rest on their bosoms.
> Loud from its rocky caverns, the deep-
> voiced neighboring ocean
> Speaks, and in accents disconsolate
> answers the wail of the forest. (61)

Compare them to those of Pratt:

> The winds of God were blowing over France,
> Kindling the hearths and altars, changing
> vows
> Of rote into an alphabet of flame.
> The air was charged with song beyond the
> range
> Of larks, with wings beyond the stretch of
> eagles.
> Skylines unknown to maps broke from
> the mists
> And there was laughter on the seas. With
> sound
> Of bugles from the Roman catacombs,
> The saints came back in their incarnate
> forms. (l.1-9)

Although Longfellow can be cited for mystical
anthropomorphism, giving us an Acadia of
bearded trees and a barkative ocean, there is,
nevertheless, an accent on nature and, even-

tually, on the Acadian peasantry as being
rooted within it. In contrast, Pratt gives us a
distinctly non-Canadian and otherworldly
opening: In his vision, God's spirit stirs France
to the point that, to the accompaniment
of angelic bugles out of Rome, classical
Christian-Catholic saints are reincarnated as
specifically Gallic men (and women). Here, in
Brébeuf, Pratt eyes, audaciously, evangelical
Christian France as the cradle of colonial
Canada. His audacity intensifies when we
consider that Martiniquan poet Aimé
Fernand David Césaire, whose masterpiece—
arguably, an epyllion–*Cahier d'un retour au
pays natal [Notebook of a Return to the Native
Land]*, which appeared in 1939, the year
before *Brébeuf*, showcases a Martinique
ruined and perverted by *French* racism and
imperialism, let alone its native versions of
Christianity.[8] Too, Pratt's zombified "marble
saints [who] leave / Their pedestals for chartless
seas and coasts / And the vast blunders of
the forest glooms" (l.51-53) arrive in North
America with seeming disinterest regarding
the commercial interests whose intrusion

---

[8] A typical, scathing portrait of the results of French imperialism in Martinique runs (in English translation): "Everybody
despises rue Paille. It's there that the village youth go astray.
It's there especially that the sea pours forth its garbage, dead
cats and its croaked dogs" (43).

(invasion) they are preparing by pacifying non-Christians to accept the usurpation of their lands.

Then again, the actual motive for the poem is, I hold, to promote Francophone adherence to the Canadian State's war effort versus the Axis, but there's also the probability that Pratt hoped that *Brébeuf* would cement his front-rank status among Anglo-Canadian poets. Pratt (1882-1964) was of the same generation as Pound (1885-1972) and T. S. Eliot (1888-1965), his leading American contemporaries, and so could not have avoided the vanity of considering himself summoned to establish "a Canadian voice and a narrative mode, later classified as 'documentary'" (Djwa xxii), as his contribution to national mythopoesis as a national epic poet: To render Canadian history with the force of myth, or literature, to give the common Canadian English reader *common* texts through which to appreciate, interrogate, and comprehend the nation. My epithet *common* registers the anxiety here, however, between intent and accomplishment. Pratt sought to become English Canada's all-Canadian poet, to be our Whitman, but as I will go on to elaborate, the aim is complicated by the truth that the Canadian nation is a warren of very competitive, competing narratives and communities. So, to cajole French-Canadians into supporting the Anti-Fascist War, Pratt had to translate Indigenous people into Fascists. His appeal to National Unity in the struggle against Hitler is thus undercut by his elimination of the colonial English as a subject community and by his *de facto* demonization of First Nations.

True: Pratt does advance, as mitigation, the notion that the Iroquois were not all bad, or, rather, were, really, not much worse than the Europeans, given that the latter also condone(d) and inflict(ed) torture. True: The Iroquois "[Dug] for [Brébeuf's] heart, fought for the scraps in the way of the wolves" (*Brébeuf* l.2061). But Pratt philosophizes that "Torture is characteristically a human process implying a development in self-consciousness" (qtd in Gingell 119). Thus, the most "appalling ironic incident" in the poem, Pratt alleges, occurs in "the martyrdom of Brébeuf where the Indians baptized him with boiling water repeating the baptismal formula of the Christian church. What a mixture of aboriginal instinct with sophisticated mockery" (qtd in Gingell 119). Now, let Césaire remind us of the French propensity for sadism: "Think of it! Ninety thousand dead in Madagascar! Indochina trampled underfoot, crushed to bits, assassinated, tortures brought back from the depths of the Middle Ages!" (*Discourse* 27). Pratt's complaints about Indigenous savagery are an example of—to abuse a well-known proverb—a black-robe paleface calling the redskins black. Pratt's epyllion details how Natives imprisoned and brutalized white French priests and colonists, and this experience is rendered as martyrdom and horror. Yet, Pratt ignores the truth that actual seventeenth-century *Nouvelle-France* harboured thousands of slaves, both Indigenous and African.[9] In addition, the French missionary Jogues, hounded by non-Christian Iroquois, is, upon his return to Christian Europe, "robbed by a pirate gang" (*Brébeuf* l.1431), one of, presumably, nominally Christian but definite Euro-Caucasian provenance.

In any event, the epic can seldom prove as unifying as it seeks to be because it is always beset by the subaltern's race-based irrationality. Though Pratt's *Brébeuf and His Brethren* strives to transform WWII-resistant, French-Canadian

---

[9] Historians squabble over the figure, for slavery in *Nouvelle-France* was multiracial (involving Panis Aboriginals, Negroes from throughout the Atlantic world, and then various and easily confused shades of Métis and Mulattoes). In any event, for the territory that is now Quebec, Marcel Trudel settled on a figure of "at least 4,185, of which 2,683 were Panis and 1,443 black," over 200 years (Mackey 95).

nationalism into a unifying, pan-Christian, newfangled, White-Man's-Burden missionary zeal, urging French-(and English-) Canadian combat against Axis brutes, the poem fails to escape imbrication in the vicious contradictions spelled out above. Pratt's Canadian nationalism is too British to be able to seduce French-Canadian nationalism.

PRATT'S *TOWARDS THE LAST SPIKE*

IN her *Canada and the Idea of North* (2001), scholar Sherrill E. Grace opines, "if Canada has a great epic poem, it is not Pratt's *Toward[s] the Last Spike*" (266). She continues on to state:

> As the telling of a foundational myth, *Toward[s] the Last Spike* strikes many resonant chords, and yet, although Pratt's narrative follows the railway west, *Toward[s] the Last Spike* is a Laurentian poem. Pratt's west is a hinterland to be opened by and for eastern centres of culture and trade, and his North is only there as a hostile force of Canadian Shield and muskeg to be dominated. (266)

Grace seems to fall back on the hoary notion of regionalist bias to deny Pratt his second gambit at writing a truly national epic, his celebration of the construction of the Canadian Pacific Railway westward through mountain ranges to reach British Columbia and the Pacific Ocean and thus extend the geopolitical reach of the only one-generation-old Dominion of Canada. Although Grace's disaffection may be correct, the actual critique is relatively weak, as if one were criticizing Montgomery's *Anne of Green Gables* for not being Anne of Red Deer, or Yellowknife, or Whitehorse. Grace does not bother to attend to the standard critique of Pratt's epic (or epyllion), that the poet omits the Chinese or proto-Chinese-Canadian labour that actually built the Prairies-to-the-Pacific Railway, a feat which had the *realpolitik* force of increasing the colonizing power of the federal government. Helpfully, though, Pratt's crime of omission is tut-tutted nicely by F. R. Scott's riposte, "All the Spikes but the Last":

> Where are the coolies in your poem, Ned?
> Where are the thousands from China
> who swung their picks with bare hands
>   at forty below? [....]
> …Did they get one of the 25,000,000 CPR acres? (194)

The poem concludes wickedly: "Is all Canada has to say to them written in the Chinese / Immigration Act?" (194). Scott thus names the capitalist and racist exploitation of Chinese

(-)Canadian labour, and then the racist effort to exclude Chinese as potential immigrants to Canada.[10]

Truly, Pratt seems uninterested in the vagaries of Chinese proletarians, save for the poem's mention of "Two hundred Chinese tugging at shore ropes" (l.1111) to assist a ship in fording a cataract, and soon this number is condensed into the racist epithet of the "*coolie*" (l.1139). Pratt's Orientalism excretes, as it were, a discrete form of Yellow Peril. Pratt's remedy for this racial panic is to bleach Chinese from the poem just as they are airbrushed, so to speak, from the historic photo of the last spike being driven.

Pratt declares *Towards* "a verse panorama of the struggle to build the first Canadian railway from the time of the proposed Terms of Union with British Columbia, 1870, to the hammering of the last spike in the Eagle Pass in 1885" (qtd in Gingell 145). But his heroes ain't labourers, anyway, but robber-baron capitalists, bankers, Victorian-imperialist politicians, and, essentially, White Anglo-Saxon Protestants, with a bias in favour of the Scottish variety. If the English are disappeared from *Brébeuf* as active competitors with the French in colonizing the Americas

---

[10] See James Walker, p. 27.

and converting (or killing) Indigenous peoples, Pratt omits not only Chinese, but French-Canadians—the other half of the "two founding peoples," Confederation tandem. Two Francophones are obliquely cited: There is the solo figure that is Liberal Opposition Member of Parliament Wilfrid Laurier[11] and a reference to the execution of the Métis leader Louis Riel (l.1404-1409). Rather, *Towards the Last Spike* is a celebration of Muscular Protestantism, tacit White British Supremacy, and Capitalist Derring-Do, with all the laurels granted Europeans and the chief heroism allotted Scots. Pratt himself comments that the poem begins to describe praiseworthy peoples and personalities by demonstrating "the effect of oatmeal on the Scotch blood and spirit of enterprise" (qtd in Gingell 145). To accomplish this passage, Pratt reports:

> I consulted specialists, Scotchmen
> themselves, physiologists, and
> dieticians, took over their data
> and added a few comments of my
> own. It is true that there were a
> few Americans, mainly Dutch

---

[11] Unnamed but described as "that young, tall, bilingual advocate / Who with the carriage of his syllables / Could bid an audience like an orchestra / Answer his body swaying like a reed" (l.1411-1414).

> Americans, and Englishmen and
> Irishmen, but the vast proportion
> of key men who came out in the
> [1870s and 1880s] to this land of
> opportunity were from the heather.
> (Qtd in Gingell 146)

Pratt elaborates on this *de facto* ethnic hierarchy
in another commentary:

> I knew that though Englishmen
> and Dutch Americans like
> Van Horne and great Irishmen
> like Shaughnessy were tremendous
> in the part they played [in
> constructing the railway], yet the
> majority of the leaders were
> Scotchmen. Well, how was I to deal
> with them? I thought here was a
> chance to picture the effect of oatmeal
> on the Scotch blood, brawn, and
> brain. (Qtd in Gingell 152)

Pratt also investigated "the effect of alcohol upon
the nervous system of a man who has reached
the depths of melancholy and pessimism"
(qtd in Gingell 152), a reference to Scottish-
Canadian Prime Minister John A. Macdonald,
one of the heroes of *Towards*. Pratt jests that,
to fulfill his probe, "I asked a number of Scotch-
men whose answers were given unequivocally

and with a calm professional assurance" (qtd in Gingell 152-153). This Scottish prominence guarantees that "The honour of driving the last spike at Craigellachie in the Eagle Pass was given to Donald Smith Strathcona: you may have seen the photograph" (qtd in Gingell 149). Importantly, to Pratt, "[Strathcona's] first stroke was a fumble which bent the nail. That's historical—the first time in his life, as far as one can gather, and probably the only time, this Scotchman ever fumbled" (qtd in Gingell 149). To the Scots, *Perfection*!

Daniel Coleman's *White Civility: The Literary Project of English Canada* (2006) reveals, through close readings of popular and canonical literary texts, the savvy ways in which White English-speaking Canadians, usually British and often Scottish, elevated the public stock of whiteness in North America by aligning it with Scottish Christian-capitalist virtues (thrift, invention, and toil) and with English (British) aristocratic chivalry and White-Man's-Burden imperialism. Pratt's *Towards* would fit aptly in Coleman's study of Scot-celebrating, Canadian texts; surely, its interest is in stereotypical, Scottish virtues: "the spirit of enterprise" and being "outstandingly economical" (qtd in Gingell 145 & 152).

Moreover, Pratt saw his own cultural ascent into the headship of Canadian letters as being signified by his ability to "[break] bread with cardinals and prime ministers, cabinet ministers, presidents and chancellors, high executives, industrialists, publishers and editors, professors and chairmen of boards..." (qtd in Gingell 149), thus naming most of the Caucasian elite that sits atop Canada's "Vertical Mosaic," to use sociologist John Porter's sage phrase.[12] Their power and class privilege is affirmed by several estates, principally lawyers (Porter 278), private school networks (285), upper-class-congregation churches (288), and engineering schools (304), and, of course, boards of directors, whether of corporations, universities, or charities, not to mention the more-or-less shared posts available in both politics and sports. In mass media, the punditocracy consists of the same related networks of "humanists, historians, economists" (Porter 461), and columnists, editorialists, and talking heads, who offer prognostications as well as insights into "the values of tradition or rational expediency, and thus [produce] ... conventional wisdom, a catalogue of the correct things to do" (Porter 461). How striking it is that Pratt,

---

[12] Here Pratt is fulfilling Frye's corporatist definition that the epic poet is one who "communicates as a professional man with a social function" (*Anatomy* 55).

personally, reveres—in particular, one may speculate—the Scottish-Canadian representation in the upper echelons of Canadian socio-economic and political power. If Pratt had written *Canterbury Tales*, and not Chaucer, his peasants would be plutocrats and their Holy Land would be Wall Street.

So, Pratt's national-poem project again falls victim to a racial blindness. It is fascinating that he publishes *Towards the Last Spike* just as the People's Republic of China, founded in 1949, was commencing its drive toward awesome industrialization, a process that would accord the PRC the world's largest economy by the 2020s. Far from being forgettable labourers, as they are in Pratt's poem, the Chinese are already the world-class examplars of "Scottish virtues" of "the spirit of enterprise" and being "outstandingly economical" (qtd in Gingell 145 & 152). Apparently, Pratt lionized—and demonized—the wrong groups of players and actors in *Towards*.

Still, one must ask, where are the First Nations, whose territories are being invaded and annexed to assist the expansion of White European "Canadian" power and capital? They are also a noticeable omission from the poem; they are set more or less as bystanders as their lands are grabbed, or as adjacent victims—collateral damage—connected to the suppression of the Riel Rebellion.

It is instructive to read Chinese-Canadian author Paul Yee's 2015 novel, *A Superior Man*, alongside Pratt's *Towards*. Introducing the novel, which begins as the railway is finished in 1885, Yee reclaims the word *coolie* to refer explicitly "to workers who did heavy labour for low wages, such as the Chinese who helped build railways in North America" (7). Yee's narrative treats the desire of the hero, Yang Hok, to return his half-Chinese/half-Native son to the boy's mother. The plan is fraught due to "conflicts arising from roadbuilding among the Chinese and Native peoples," and these "issues fester," for "both races were disdained as inferior by whites ('redbeards')" (back cover). Yee rejects replicating Pratt's Big Nation Chauvinism or what Glen Sean Coulthard sums up as "the reproduction of the colonial relationship between Indigenous peoples and what [became] Canada [depending] heavily on the deployment of state power geared around genocidal practices of forced *exclusion* and *assimilation*" (4). Rather than participate in the forced disappearance of Indigenous people from grassland, mountain, and coast, or the degradation of Chinese, Yee unites both groups, to put forward an alternative narrative of Indigenous struggle and minority / immigrant repression that could serve as a new paradigm through which to understand the coming into being of contemporary Canada.

No wonder, then, that the one section of Pratt's *Towards the Last Spike* that is unabashedly enjoyable is his depiction of the land itself:

> On the North Shore a reptile lay asleep—
> A hybrid that the myths might have conceived,
> But not delivered, as progenitor
> Of crawling, gliding things upon the earth.
> She lay snug in the folds of a huge boa
> Whose tail had covered Labrador and swished
> Atlantic tides, whose body coiled itself
> Around the Hudson Bay, then curled up north
> Through Manitoba and Saskatchewan
> To Great Slave Lake. In continental reach
> The neck went past the Great Bear Lake until
> Its head was hidden in the Arctic Seas.
> (*Towards* l.870-881)

The land is itself the indomitable villain in the piece, which makes Pratt's poem something of a piece with Earle Birney's warning about too blithely encountering the Canadian wilderness, namely, "David" (1942). Birney's poem also humanizes geological formations: "The peak was upthrust / Like a fist in a frozen ocean of rock…" (229). Just as Pratt seems to have sought to match, in *Brébeuf*, Longfellow's eventual, Francophone success with *Evangeline*, so might *Towards the Last Spike* constitute an attempt to equal or surpass Birney's achievement in *"David."*[13]

But errors are impossible to avoid for the would-be national, Canadian poet: How can one craft a poem that is truly representative of the variegated whole that is Canada, with provinces and territories and First Nations and multicultures, all as jealously distinct as any ecosystem? To his credit, Ned Pratt tried, but by siding with empowered elites (whatever the reason), Pratt served up fairy

[13] If any long poem in Canada deserves the title of "national epic," it might very well be "David," given that, as Al Purdy wrote, 45 years ago, "A GENERATION of Canadian schoolchildren and university students has grown up knowing the story of a mountain climber who fell 50 feet to a narrow ledge, was badly injured, then pushed off the ledge to his death by his friend in an act of mercy. The climber's name was David, also the title of the story. Its author was Earle Birney" ("The Man Who Killed David"). Furthermore, "At one time or another in the last 25 years, 'David' has been required reading for high schools and universities in every Canadian province" ("The Man Who Killed David").

tales of progress as opposed to weighing histories of repression. He sought a "national" nationalism, but both his Francophone and Anglophone subjects seemed too parochial, too ethnic-ghettoized, to survive the forensic scrutiny of later generations of multicultural-ized and/or Indigenous / Métis Canadian poets and scholars. Pratt's imagined Canada is intended to lionize French Catholic martyr-priests and parsimonious-prosperous Scot capitalists, to hold up these figures as mythical, as worthy of mass adulation and emulation. But, well, not so fast!

In *The Wretched of the Earth*, the Martiniquan-Algerian theorist of post-colonial liberation, Frantz Fanon, posits, "The national government, …to be national, ought to govern by the people and for the people, for the outcasts and by the outcasts" (205). The same must hold true for the would-be "national poet." Pitch your tale to the outcasts, and you are more likely to author a meaningful, national text. Write for elites, and you ink highfalutin propaganda. Damnation!

WORKS CITED

Birney, Earle. "David." 1942. *Poetry of Our Time: An Introduction to Twentieth-Century Poetry, Including Modern Canadian Poetry.* Ed. Louis Dudek. Toronto: Macmillan, 1966. 229-237. Print.

Camões, Luís Vaz de. *The Lusiads.* 1572. Trans. William C. Atkinson. London: Penguin, 1952. Print.

Césaire, Aimé. *Cahier d'un retour au pays natal. 1939. [Notebook of a Return to the Native Land.] Aimé Césaire: The Collected Poetry.* Trans. Clayton Eshleman and Annette Smith. Berkeley: University of California Press, 1983. 32-85. Print.

-----. *Discourse on Colonialism.* Trans: Joan Pinkham. New York: Monthly Review Press, 1972. Print.

Chaucer, Geoffrey. *The Canterbury Tales.* 1372-1400. Print.

Clarke, George Elliott. "Why Not an 'African-Canadian' Epic? Lessons from Pratt and Walcott." *Comparative Literature for the New Century*. Eds. Giulia de Gasperi and Joseph Pivato. Kingston (ON) & Montreal: McGill-Queen's University Press, 2018. 117-152. Print.

Coleman, Daniel. *White Civility: The Literary Project of English Canada*. Toronto: University of Toronto Press, 2006. Print.

"Conscription Crisis of 1917." By Wikipedia contributors. *Wikipedia, The Free Encyclopedia*. March 16, 2018. Electronic. https://en.wikipedia.org/wiki/Conscription_Crisis_of_1917

Coulthard, Glen Sean. *Red Skin, White Masks: Rejecting the Colonial Politics of Recognition*. Minneapolis: University of Minnesota Press, 2014. Print.

Djwa, Sandra, ed. "Editors' Introduction." *Selected Poems*. By E. J. Pratt. Eds. Sandra Djwa, W. J. Keith, and Zailig Pollock. Toronto: University of Toronto Press, 2000. [ix]-xxii. Print.

Fanon, Frantz. *Black Skin, White Masks*. 1952. Trans. Charles Lam Markmann. New York: Grove Press, 1967. Print.

-----. *The Wretched of the Earth*. 1961. Trans. Constance Farrington. New York: Grove Press, 1968. Print.

Frye, Northrop. *Anatomy of Criticism: Four Essays*. Princeton: Princeton University Press, 1957. Print.

-----. "Canada and Its Poetry" (1943). Dudek and Gnarowski, eds. *The Making of Modern Poetry in Canada: Essential Articles on Contemporary Canadian Poetry in English*. 1967. Toronto: The Ryerson Press, 1970. 86-97. Print.

Gingell, Susan, ed. *The Collected Works of E. J. Pratt: E. J. Pratt on His Life and Poetry*. Toronto: University of Toronto Press, 1983. Print.

Godbout, Patricia. *Brébeuf et ses frères: A French translation of Brébeuf and His Brethren* by E. J. Pratt. M.A. Thesis, Université de Sherbrooke, 1988. Electronic. http://savoirs.usherbrooke.ca/handle/11143/10347

Grace, Sherrill E. *Canada and the Idea of North*. Montreal-Kingston: McGill-Queen's University Press, 2001. Print.

Harper, Philip Brian. "Nationalism and Social Division in Black Arts Poetry of the 1960s." *Critical Inquiry*. 19.2 (Winter 1993): 234-255. Print.

Homer. *The Iliad*. 760-710 B.C. Trans. Robert Fagles. New York: Penguin, 1998. Print.

-----. *The Odyssey*. 800-760 B.C. Trans. Robert Fitzgerald. Garden City, NY: Doubleday, 1961. Print.

The Kalevala. Ed. & comp., Elias Lönnrot. 1849. Trans. Keith Bosley. Oxford: Oxford University Press, 1999, 2008. Print.

Kipling, Rudyard. "The White Man's Burden." *The New York Sun*. 10 February 1899. Print.

LeMay, Pamphile. *Évangéline*. 1865. Print.

Longfellow, Henry Wadsworth. *Evangeline [And the Evangeline Country]*. 1847. Toronto: Collins, 1947. 61-188. Print.

-----. *The Song of Hiawatha*. 1855. Print.

Mackey, Frank. *Done with Slavery: The Black Fact in Montreal*. Montreal-Kingston: McGill-Queen's University Press, 2010. Print.

Montgomery, Lucy Maud. *Anne of Green Gables*. Boston: L. C. Page & Co., 1908. Print.

Moody, A. David. *Ezra Pound: Poet, I: The Young Genius 1885-1920*. New York: Oxford University Press, 2007. Print.

Nadeau, Jean-François. *Adrien Arcand: Führer Canadien*. Montréal: Lux Éditeur, 2010. Print.

Pitt, David G. *E. J. Pratt: The Truant Years,
    1882-1927*. St. John's—Toronto:
    University of Toronto Press—Jesperson
    Press, 1984. Print.

Porter, John. *The Vertical Mosaic: An Analysis
    of Social Class and Power in Canada*.
    1965. Toronto: University of Toronto
    Press, 2015. Print.

Pound, Ezra. *The Cantos*. Fourth Collection
    Edition. London: Faber & Faber, 1987.
    Print.

-----. *The Pisan Cantos*. Ed. Richard Sieburth.
    1948. New York: New Directions, 2003.
    Print.

-----. "Three Cantos." *Poetry*. 10.3 (June
    1917): 113-254. Print.

Pratt, E. J. *Brébeuf and His Brethren*. 1940.
    E. J. Pratt: Complete Poems: Part 2.
    Eds. Sandra Djwa, and R. G. Moyles.
    Toronto: University of Toronto Press,
    1989. 46-110. Print.

-----. "From Java to Geneva." [Later entitled,
    "From Stone to Steel."] *Anthology of
    Canadian Poetry (English)*. Ed. Ralph
    Gustafson. Harmondsworth: Penguin—
    Pelican, 1942. 58-59. Print.

-----. "From Java to Geneva." [Later entitled
    "From Stone to Steel."] *New Provinces:
    Poems of Several Authors*. By E. J. Pratt, et
    al. 1936. Toronto: University of Toronto
    Press, 1976. 44. Print.

-----. "From Stone to Steel." *E. J. Pratt: Complete Poems, Part 1*. Eds. Sandra Djwa and R. G. Moyles. Toronto: University of Toronto Press, 1989. 260-261. Print.

-----. *Towards the Last Spike*. 1952. *E. J. Pratt: Complete Poems: Part 2*. Eds. Sandra Djwa and R. G. Moyles. Toronto: University of Toronto Press, 1989. 201-250. Print.

Purdy, Al. "The Man Who Killed David." 1974. Electronic. https://www.tru.ca/arts/e_birney/english/level3/level4/doc00701.htm

"Ralph Gustafson." By Wikipedia contributors. *Wikipedia, The Free Encyclopedia*. March 17, 2018. Electronic. https://en.wikipedia.org/wiki/Ralph_Gustafson

Scott, F. R. "All the Spikes but the Last." *The Collected Poems of F. R. Scott*. Toronto: McClelland and Stewart, 1981. 194. Print.

Stoicheff, Peter. *The Hall of Mirrors*: Drafts & Fragments *and the End of Ezra Pound's* Cantos. Ann Arbor: University of Michigan Press, 1995. Print.

Whitman, Walt. *Leaves of Grass*. 1855. Mineola, NY: Dover Publications, 2007. Print.

Yee, Paul. *A Superior Man*. Vancouver, BC: Arsenal Pulp Press, 2015. Print.

PERMISSIONS AND ACKNOWLEDGMENTS

Portions of George Elliott Clarke's public lecture—*The Quest for a "National" Nationalism: E. J. Pratt's Epic Ambition, "Race" Consciousness, and the Contradictions of Canadian Identity*—first appeared in "Why Not an 'African-Canadian' Epic? Lessons from Pratt and Walcott," in *Comparative Literature for the New Century*, eds. Giulia de Gasperi and Joseph Pivato, Kingston (ON) & Montreal: McGill-Queen's University Press, 2018. pp. 117-152. Reprinted with permission of editors Giulia de Gasperi and Joseph Pivato.

We essayed conscientiously to contact all essential rights holders.

Excerpts from "Editors' Introduction," by Sandra Djwa, in *E. J. Pratt: Selected Poems*, edited by Sandra Djwa, W. J. Keith, and Zailig Pollock © University of Toronto Press 2000.

I must acknowledge here the consummately collegial devotion of Prof. Andrew Loman, of the Department of English at Memorial University of Newfoundland, in, first, inviting my lecture in March 2018 and assisting me in finding some essential sources, and then securing the presentation's publication by Memorial University of Newfoundland and Breakwater Books. Prof. Loman is a gifted scholar and academic impresario, gently nudging me along, over three years, to complete the research and writing, the editing, and, painstakingly, the search for copyright holders. I thank him profoundly for his camaraderie and his patience, his deft editing and uplifting humour.

I also acknowledge the great patience and careful editing practised by Breakwater Books, specifically Rebecca Rose and Jocelyne Thomas. I thank Breakwater, also, for reviving the tradition of printing the Pratt Memorial Lecture.

Although my article is properly critical of Ned Pratt's socio-political stance, he was yet a mighty poet, and his epics remain requisite models for other Canadian poets. Instructively, his epyllion *The Titanic* (1935) is, irrefutably, a masterpiece. I am proud to bear his name as the inaugural E. J. Pratt Professor of Canadian Literature—a title that may only be held by a professor who is also a poet—at the University of Toronto. Thus, I thank the backers of the Pratt "Chair," namely, Dr. Sonia Labatt, PhD, and Victoria University (a college of the University of Toronto), where, in fact, Ned Pratt taught and where many of his papers are held.

Finally, I thank my companion, the excellent poet Giovanna Riccio, for her bounties of grace and cheer, enlightenment and charity, compassion and inspiration. She enters into writing as a cathedral for solo contemplation and then, eventually, joyous communion, and I strive to be a disciple of such illuminated discipline.

George Elliott Clarke

GEORGE **ELLIOTT** CLARKE

The 4TH Poet Laureate of Toronto (2012-15) and the 7TH Parliamentary/Canadian Poet Laureate (2016-17), George Elliott Clarke was born in Windsor, Nova Scotia, in 1960. Educated at the University of Waterloo, Dalhousie University, and Queen's University, Clarke is also a pioneering scholar of African-Canadian literature, with two major tomes to his credit: *Odysseys Home: Mapping African-Canadian Literature* (2002) and *Directions Home: Approaches to African-Canadian Literature* (2012). A professor of English at the University of Toronto, Clarke has taught at Duke, McGill, the University of British Columbia, and Harvard. He holds eight honourary doctorates, plus appointments to the Order of Nova Scotia and the Order of Canada at the rank of Officer. He is also a Fellow of the Royal Canadian Geographical Society. His recognitions include the Pierre Elliott Trudeau Fellows Prize, the Governor-General's Award for Poetry, the National Magazine Gold Award for Poetry, the Premiul Poesis (Romania), the Dartmouth Book Award for Fiction, the Eric Hoffer Book Award for Poetry (US), and the Dr. Martin Luther King Jr. Achievement Award. He has titles available in Chinese, Italian, and Romanian.